Commentaries

on

Silo's Message

Commentaries

on

Silo's Message

Latitude Press

Published by Latitude Press
www.latitudepress.com
ISBN 978-1-878977-46-5
Printed in the USA
First edition A

Information on Silo's Message
www.silosmessage.net

These Commentaries do not cover all of the topics in *Silo's Message,* but only those that seem necessary for a better understanding of this writing.

We will approach *Silo's Message* respecting the order of that exposition. Therefore, the first part will be devoted to the chapters and paragraphs of the book *The Inner Look;* the second part will consider "The Experience;" and the third, "The Path."

CONTENTS

First Part of *Silo's Message*

THE BOOK

The Inner Look

In the first part we will comment on The Book, *The Inner Look*, and consider the **first three chapters**, which are introductory and refer to certain precautions that should be taken in order to correctly frame the most important themes.

Until **Chapter V** the text provides explanations against a background of non-meaning that the seeker of more definitive truths will feel inclined to dismiss. There we find chapters and paragraphs that deserve some consideration. But first we must ask ourselves: What does The Book aspire to convey? It tries to transmit a teaching about conduct and about human interiority, with reference to meaning in life.

Why does The Book have the title *The Inner Look*? Isn't the organ of sight placed so as to glimpse the outside world, like a window, or two, if that were the case; isn't the eye located so as to open each day upon the awakening of the consciousness? The back of the eye receives the impacts of the external world. But sometimes, when I close my eyes, I remember the outside world, or I imagine it, or I daydream about it, or I dream it. I see this world with an inner eye which also looks at a screen, but not one that corresponds to the external world.

To mention an "inner look" is to imply someone who looks and a something that is looked at. This is what The Book is about, and its title foreshadows an unexpected confrontation with that which is accepted naively. The title of The Book summarizes these ideas: "There are other things that are seen with other eyes, and there is an observer that can be positioned in a way that is different from the habitual." We must now make a small distinction.

When I say, "I see something," I announce that I'm in a passive attitude with respect to a phenomenon that strikes my eyes. When, however, I say that, "I *look* at something," I'm announcing that I direct my eyes in a certain direction. Almost in the same sense, I can speak of "inner seeing," of attending to internal scenes such as those of divagation or dreams, distinguishing the "inner look" as an active direction of my consciousness. In this way, I can remember my dreams, or my life, or my fantasies, and look at them actively, illuminating them in their apparent absurdity, seeking to give them meaning.

The inner look is an active direction of the consciousness. It is a direction that seeks significance and meaning in the apparently confusing and chaotic inner world. This direction is previous to that look; it impels it. It is this direction that permits the activity of looking internally. And if you manage to grasp that the inner look is necessary to reveal the meaning that impels it, you will understand that in some moment the you who looks will have to see yourself. This "yourself" or "oneself" is not the look or even the consciousness. This "self" is what gives meaning to the look and the operations of the consciousness. It is previous and transcendent to the consciousness itself. In a very broad fashion we will call this "self," "Mind," in order not to confuse it with the operations of the consciousness, or with the consciousness itself. But when someone seeks to apprehend the Mind as though it were simply one more phenomenon of the consciousness, it will escape them, for it admits neither representation nor comprehension.

The inner look will have to collide with the meaning that the Mind gives to all phenomena, even one's own consciousness and one's own life, and the collision with this meaning will illuminate the consciousness and life. This is what The Book addresses in its most profound nucleus.

All of the above leads us to reflect on the title of the work. As we enter The Book, the first paragraph of the first chapter tells us: "Here it tells how the non-meaning of life can be converted into meaning and fulfillment." And paragraph five of the same chapter explains: "Here it tells of the inner revelation at which all arrive who carefully meditate in humble search."

The objective is set: To convert the non-meaning of life into meaning. Moreover, the way is outlined to reach the revelation of meaning, based on careful meditation.

Entering the material:

Chapter I develops the way to reach inner revelation, cautioning against false attitudes that lead one away from the proposed objective.

Chapter III deals with what has been called "the non-meaning." The development of this chapter begins with the paradox of "triumph-failure" in these terms: "Those who bore failure in their hearts were able to illuminate the final victory, while those who felt triumphant were left by the wayside, vegetating in their muted and diffuse life."

In this chapter, "failure" is vindicated as non-compliance with the temporary meanings in life and a state of dissatisfaction that drives definitive searches. The chapter highlights the danger of enchantment with the temporary triumphs of life, those that if achieved simply demand more, and lead finally to disappointment; and if not achieved still lead to definitive disappointment, to skepticism, and to nihilism.

Further on in the same chapter but still in the first paragraph it states: "There is no meaning in life if everything ends with death." However, it remains to be demonstrated whether life does or does not end with death, on the one hand, and whether life does or does not have meaning as a function of the fact of death... Resolution of these double questions, which are beyond the field of Logic, is approached throughout the book in terms of existence. Be that as it may, this first paragraph of **Chapter III** is not something to be read quickly, immediately moving on to the next paragraph. It calls for a pause and some reflection, since it involves a central point of Doctrine. The following paragraphs in the chapter highlight the relativity of human values and actions.

Chapter IV considers all the factors of dependence that operate on the human being, diminishing possibilities of choice and free action.

Chapter V deals with the appearance of certain states of consciousness whose character is different from the habitual. They involve suggestive phenomena which are not thereby extraordinary, but that in any case have the virtue of awakening intimations of a new meaning in life. This intimation of meaning, while far from giving one faith, or promoting belief, is something that can change or relativize a skeptical denial of meaning in life.

The register of such phenomena does not go beyond provoking intellectual doubt, but does, through that character of experience, have the advantage of affecting the subject in daily life. In this sense, it has greater capacity for transformation than a theory or set of ideas, which would simply change the point of view regarding a given position toward life.

This chapter touches on certain events which, whether true or not from an objective point of view, place the subject in a mental situation that is different from the habitual. These events have the capacity to present themselves along with intuitions that make one suspect there is another way of living reality. And it is precisely this "suspicion" of another kind of reality that opens us to other horizons. In every age, so-called "miracles" (in the sense of phenomena contrary to normal perception) bring with them intuitions that place the subject in another mental ambit. To this other ambit, which we call "inspired consciousness," we attribute numerous meanings and correlatively many expressions.

The paragraphs of this chapter configure a kind of incomplete but adequate list of registers which, when they occur, invariably give rise to questions about the meaning of life. Their register is of such psychic intensity that it demands answers in relation to their meaning. And whatever the answers, the intimate flavor they leave is always an intimation of a different reality.

Let's consider the cases: "At times I have anticipated events that later took place. At times I have grasped a distant thought. At times I have described places I have never been. At times I have recounted exactly what took place in my absence. At times an immense joy has surprised me. At times a total comprehension has overwhelmed me. At times a perfect communion with everything has filled me with ecstasy. At times I have broken through my reveries and seen reality in a new way. At times I have seen something for the first time, yet recognized it as though I had seen it before. …And all this has made me think. It is clear to me that without these experiences I could not have emerged from the non-meaning."

Chapter VI establishes differences between the states of sleep, semi-sleep, and vigil. The intention is placed on showing the relative nature of the idea that people normally have about everyday reality, and about the accuracy of that perceived reality.

Chapters VII, VIII, IX, X, XI, XII, and later **chapters XV, XVI, XVII,** and **XVIII** deal, directly or indirectly, with the phenomenon of The Force.

The theme of The Force is of the utmost interest because it gives us a practical way to put in motion experiences that orient us toward meaning. This is different from the experiences mentioned in chapter V that, although they provide an intimation of meaning, occur spontaneously or without any particular direction. At the end of these commentaries on *The Inner Look* we will deal with the subject of The Force and its implications.

For now we will concentrate on the four remaining chapters of The Book.

Chapter XIII sets forth "The Principles of Valid Action." It deals with the formulation of a behavior in life that is presented for those who wish to develop a coherent life built on two basic internal registers: that of unity and that of contradiction.

In this way, the justification for this "morality" is found in the registers that it produces, and not in particular ideas or beliefs tied to one place, time, or cultural model. The register of internal unity that is being sought is accompanied by certain indicators to take into account. These are:

1. The sensation of internal growth
2. Continuity in time
3. Affirming that one would want to repeat it in the future

The sensation of internal growth appears as a true and positive indicator that always accompanies the experience of personal improvement.

Regarding continuity in time, it means that through comparison with later, or imagined, or remembered situations, one is able to confirm that the validity of the experience does not change, even with changing circumstances.

Lastly, if after the act one wishes to repeat it, we can say that the sensation of internal unity affirms the validity of this action. On the contrary, contradictory actions might have some of the characteristics of unitive actions, or none of them, but they never have all three.

There exist, nevertheless, actions of another type that we cannot strictly call "valid," but neither can we call them "contradictory." While such actions do not prevent our development, they do not produce great improvement either.

These actions can be more or less disagreeable or more or less pleasurable, but from the point of view of validity they neither add nor take anything away. Such actions are the everyday actions, the mechanically habitual actions. They are perhaps necessary for our subsistence and coexistence. But according to the model of unitive and contradictory actions that we have been examining, such an action does not in itself constitute a moral act.

The Principles, referred to as "The Principles of Valid Action," are classified as:

1. The Principle of Adaptation
2. The Principle of Action and Reaction
3. The Principle of Opportune Action
4. The Principle of Proportion
5. The Principle of Acceptance
6. The Principle of Pleasure
7. The Principle of Immediate Action
8. The Principle of Comprehended Action
9. The Principle of Liberty
10. The Principle of Solidarity
11. The Principle of Negation of Opposites
12. The Principle of Accumulation of Actions

Chapter XIV of The Book is about the "Guide to the Inner Road." This Guide has no greater pretensions than any other guided experience, although it is framed within practices proposed in a transcendental direction that are "suggestive" or give an "intimation of meaning."

Chapter XIX talks about the "internal states." This chapter is not a guided experience and it does not claim to hold transferential solutions. Instead it tries, in an allegorical way, to describe present situations in which readers may find themselves.

This chapter is a poetic and allegorical description of various situations in which a person can find themselves while on their path toward the encounter with the meaning of life. As its first paragraph states: "You must now gain sufficient insight into the various internal states you may find yourself in throughout the course of your life, particularly in the course of your evolutionary work."

Here we understand "evolutionary work" as that which permits one to clear up unknowns in the development of the meaning of life.

Chapter XX, titled "Internal Reality," is a little obscure. Its interpretation appears difficult for those who are not familiar with the theory of symbols and allegories and the phenomena of production, translation, and deformation of impulses. In any case, and leaving aside the theoretical comprehension of this final chapter, it is not difficult to find people who can perceive with relative clarity their internal states and are able to grasp those meanings on a profound level, as they would that of any poetic phrase.

Returning now to the chapters related to the Force: The themes of the Force, the Luminous Center, the

Internal Light, the Double, and the Projection of the Energy, admit two different views.

First, we can consider them as phenomena of personal experience, and therefore tend not to discuss them with people who have not registered them, or in the best of cases limit ourselves to more or less subjective descriptions.

Secondly, we can consider them within a larger theory that can explain them, without appealing to the test of subjective experience. Such a theory derived from a Transcendental Psychology* is of a complexity and profundity that make it impossible to deal with in these simple "Commentaries on Silo's Message."

---

* See Psychology IV in *Psychology Notes* by Silo, www.silo.net and forthcoming from Latitude Press.

Second Part of *Silo's Message*

THE EXPERIENCE

Ceremonies

In this second part, called "The Experience," we consider eight ceremonies that are provided for different cases and situations of personal and social life.

In almost all of these ceremonies there are two realities present that, whether treated explicitly or not, show their importance through the profound significance that they have for life. We know these realities, which allow for different interpretations, by the designations "Immortality" and "the Sacred."

The Message gives the greatest importance to these themes, and explains that everyone must have the full right to believe or not to believe in Immortality and the Sacred, because the orientation of a person's life will depend on how they place themselves in relation to these themes.

The Message acknowledges the difficulties of openly examining these fundamental beliefs, confronting the censorship and self-censorship that inhibit free thought and good conscience.

In the context of free interpretation that The Message favors, it is accepted that for some, immortality refers to actions carried out in life, but whose effects continue in the physical world despite physical death. For others, it is the memories retained by loved ones, by groups, or even society, that ensure continuation after physical death. For still others, immortality is accepted as personal continuity on another level, in another "landscape" of existence.

Continuing with the subject of freedom of interpretation, some sense the Sacred as the engine of their deepest affection. For them, their children or other loved ones represent the Sacred and have the highest value, something that should not be disparaged for any reason. Some consider human beings and their universal rights as Sacred. Others experience divinity as the essence of the Sacred.

In the communities that are formed around the Message, it is assumed that the different positions in facing Immortality and the Sacred should not merely be "tolerated" but genuinely respected.

The sacred manifests from the depths of the human being, hence the importance of the experience of the Force, as an extraordinary phenomenon that we can cause to erupt into the everyday world. Without experience everything is doubtful; with the experience of the Force we have profound evidence. We do not need faith to recognize the Sacred. The Force is obtained in ceremonies such as the Service and Laying on of Hands, and in the ceremonies of Well-Being and Assistance we can also perceive the effects of the Force.

Contact with the Force causes an acceleration of and increase in psychophysical energy; this is especially true if coherent acts are realized daily, something which also creates internal unity oriented toward spiritual growth.

The first experience is known as the "Service." This is a social ceremony that is performed at the request of a group of people. Two participants, referred to as the "Officiant" and the "Assistant," establish a kind of dialogue, which allows everyone to follow the same steps from beginning to end.

This is an experience that makes use of particular forms of relaxation, which in a short while give way to a set of visual and cenesthetic images that ultimately take the form of a moving "spherical shape," capable of unleashing the Force. At one point, the Assistant reads a Principle or a thought from *The Inner Look* as a theme for meditation. Finally, the participants make an Asking in the direction of what each one experiences as their deepest "need."

Another social ceremony is known as the "Laying on of Hands." It works with the register of the Force more directly than in the Service. Here we do not make use of the evocation or the register of the sphere. Neither do we read a Principle or suggest a theme for meditation. The same mechanism of the Asking is maintained as in the ceremony of the Service.

A third ceremony is known as "Well-Being." It is carried out at the request of the participants. This ceremony involves adopting a mental position in which participants evoke one or more people, trying to remember as vividly as possible their presence and their most characteristic affective tone. We seek to comprehend, in the most intense possible way, the difficulties they may be experiencing at this moment. We then go on to focus on an improvement in their situation in order that a corresponding register of relief is experienced.

This ceremony highlights a mechanism of "best wishes" or "good intentions," with which we frequently express ourselves almost spontaneously. We say, "Have a good day," "Happy birthday to you, and many more," "I hope your test goes well," or "I hope everything turns out well," etc. It is clear that in this ceremony the "Asking" is done with a good mental disposition, where the emphasis is on intense affective registers. This "Asking" of benefit for others, performed in the best conditions, puts us in a mental position where we are predisposed to give the necessary help; it also improves our mental direction and increases the possibilities of communication with others.

A very important point to consider in relation to the "Askings" is to carry them out so that others can overcome their difficulties and reestablish their best possibilities. There should be no confusion about this. Let us consider an example. One might assume that in the case of someone who is dying, an Asking for the recovery of their health is the most appropriate thing, since we are trying to diminish the person's pain and suffering. But we must be careful how we focus the Asking, because it is not a question of asking for what is best for ourselves, who want to keep that person in good health and close to us. The correct Asking should aim at what is best for the dying person and not what is best for us. In this situation, where we are emotionally attached to that person who is suffering and dying, perhaps we should also consider that the person may wish to leave that situation, reconciled and at peace with him or herself. In this case, the Asking is for "the best for the affected person" and not what is best for me, who wants to hold on to that person at all costs. So, in Asking for others I must consider what is best for them, and not for me.

This ceremony ends with the opportunity, for those present who wish, to feel the presence of loved ones who, "although not present here, in our time and in our space," are related to us, or have related to us, in an experience of love, peace, and warm joy.

Finally, this ceremony attempts to create a current of well-being for all those present, who are oriented in the same direction.

The fourth ceremony is called "Protection." For this ceremony the Officiant and Assistant gather with the relatives and friends of the children to whom it is dedicated. Explanations about formalities and meanings are given throughout the course of this ceremony of change of state.

The fifth ceremony is that of "Marriage."
Also social in nature, this ceremony is usually celebrated with the participation of many couples who wish to join together and give public testimony of their change of status. As in the ceremony Protection, throughout the ceremony there are explanations about formalities and meanings.

The sixth ceremony is called "Assistance."
It is carried out for an individual. As explained in the preamble to the words of the Officiant: "This is a ceremony of great affection. It requires the person performing it to give the best of him or herself. The ceremony may be repeated at the request of the person receiving it or those caring for him or her. The Officiant is alone with the dying person. Regardless of whether the person who is dying appears lucid or unconscious, the Officiant comes close to them and speaks slowly in a voice that is soft and clear."

Many of the phrases read by the Officiant are from chapter XIV of *The Inner Look,* "Guide to the Inner Road." The sequences, images, and allegories that are presented have the structure of a profound guided experience.

The seventh ceremony is that of "Death." As in the ceremony of Assistance, it is carried out by an Officiant. However, it is a social ceremony for family, friends, and acquaintances of the deceased.

The eighth and final ceremony is called "Recognition." It is carried out by an Officiant and an Assistant. The preamble of the ceremony explains that it is a ceremony of inclusion in the Community, "...*inclusion through common experiences, shared ideals, attitudes, and common procedures. The ceremony is carried out at the request of a group of people and following a Service. Those who will participate should have the written text.*" This ceremony has the structure of a collective testimony.

Third Part of *Silo's Message*

THE PATH

This third part presents seventeen themes of meditation. They are related to achieving coherence in one's thinking, feeling, and doing. This work that one carries out to advance toward coherence, toward unity in life, and away from contradiction and disintegration of life, is called "The Path." We group the seventeen topics into two blocks:

In the block of the first eight themes we are shown the situation of one who seeks coherence and also the way to advance toward that coherence.

In the block of the last nine items we are shown the difficulties that must be avoided in order to advance toward coherence.

1. *"If you believe that your life will end with death, nothing that you think, feel, or do has any meaning. Everything will end with incoherence and disintegration."*

What is being declared here is that no justification is possible from within the perspective of death. Furthermore, we live our lives moved by our vital needs. Eating, drinking, defending ourselves from the aggression of nature, the search for pleasure, are all major impulses that allow for the continuity of life in the short term. Thanks to the illusion of life's permanence we are able to maintain all of our activities, but they cannot be justified outside of this illusion of permanence.

2. *"If you believe that your life does not end with death, you must bring into agreement what you think with what you feel and what you do. All must advance toward coherence, toward unity."*

This affirms that in the case of belief in the permanence or projection of life beyond death, such justification can be found through making thinking, feeling, and acting coincide in the same direction. Life can continue or be projected through a type of dynamic unity, and in no case through contradiction.

3. "If you are indifferent to the pain and suffering of others, none of the help that you ask for will find justification."

In the world of relationships there can be no justification for one's own needs while denying the needs of others.

4. "If you are not indifferent to the pain and suffering of others then in order to help them you must bring your thoughts, feelings, and actions into agreement."

A coherent position in the face of the pain and suffering of others demands that our thoughts, feelings, and actions coincide in the same direction.

5. "Learn to treat others in the way that you want to be treated."

If we intend for our world of relationships to be coherent, it must be governed by reciprocity of actions. This position is not "naturally given" in behavior, but is considered something that grows, something that must be learned. This behavior is known as "the Golden Rule." It is learned and perfected over time and experience in the world of relationships.

6. *"Learn to surpass pain and suffering in yourself, in those close to you, and in human society."*

Rather than resigning oneself to one's supposed human "nature," learning is also possible here. That learning extends to others as a result of lessons learned in overcoming one's own suffering.

7. *"Learn to resist the violence that is within you and outside of you."*

As the foundation of all learning about overcoming and coherence.

8. *"Learn to recognize the signs of the sacred within you and around you."*

This intuition of the "Sacred," of that which is irreplaceable, grows and spreads to different fields until it ends up orienting one's life (the Sacred in oneself) and one's actions in life (the Sacred outside of oneself).

---

9. *"Do not let your life pass by without asking yourself, 'Who am I?'"*

In the sense of the meanings of one's self and that which distorts what is referred to as "one's self."

10. *"Do not let your life pass by without asking yourself, 'Where am I going?'"*

In the sense of your life's direction and goals.

11. *"Do not let a day pass by without giving an answer to yourself about who you are."*

A daily reminder of one's own relation to finitude.

12. *"Do not let a day pass by without giving an answer to yourself about where you are going."*

This is the daily remembering of oneself in relation to the objectives and direction of one's own life.

13. *"Do not let a great joy pass without giving thanks internally."*

Not only because of the importance of recognizing a great joy, but also because of the positive disposition which the "thanking" accentuates, reinforcing the importance of what is being experienced.

14. *"Do not let a great sadness pass without calling into your interior for the joy that you have saved there."*

If at those precise moments we were conscious of these experiences of joy, we can later evoke them in difficult moments by calling on the memory ("charged" with positive emotions). One might think that in this "comparison" you will lose the positive state, but that is not the case, because this "comparison" allows you to modify the affective inertia of the negative states.

15. *"Do not imagine that you are alone in your village, in your city, on the Earth, or among the infinite worlds."*

We experience this "loneliness" as "abandonment" by other intentions and ultimately as being "abandoned" by the future. Speaking of "your village, your city, the Earth and the infinite worlds" confronts each and every one of those locations, small or large, unpopulated or populated, with the loneliness and negation of all possible intention.

The opposite position starts from one's own intention and extends beyond the time and space that elapses for our perception and memory. We are accompanied by diverse intentions, and even in the apparent cosmic solitude there exists "something." There is something that manifests its presence.

16. *"Do not imagine that you are enchained to this time and this space."*

If you cannot imagine or perceive another time and another space, you can intuit an internal space and time in which the experiences of other "landscapes" operate. In these intuitions you surpass the determinism of time and space. This is a matter of experiences that are not linked to either perception or memory. These experiences are recognized only indirectly, and only when "entering" or "leaving" these spaces and these times. These intuitions occur through the displacement of the "I," and their beginning and end can be recognized by a new accommodation of the "I." The direct intuition of these "landscapes" (in those profound spaces) is dimly remembered through temporal contexts, never by "objects" of perception or representation.

17. *"Do not imagine that in your death loneliness will become eternal."*

Considering death as "nothingness" or as utter solitude, it is clear that the "before" and "after" of this profound experience do not subsist. The Mind transcends the consciousness that is linked to the "I" and to the times and spaces of perception and representation. Nevertheless, nothing that happens in the profound spaces can be made evident in experience.

> *Silo*
> Center of Studies
> Parks of Study and Reflection
> Punta de Vacas
> March 3, 2009

For information on
Communities of Silo's Message
www.silosmessage.net

For information on the book
Silo's Message see
www.silo.net
www.latitudepress.com